# TO MAKE A
# BABY LAUGH

## JACK MOORE

PHOTOGRAPHS BY PENNY GENTIEU

WORKMAN PUBLISHING · NEW YORK

Library of Congress Cataloging-in-Publication Data is available.

ISBN 978-0-7611-7235-2

Design: Janet Vicario

Workman books are available at special discounts when purchased
in bulk for premiums and sales promotions as well as for fund-raising
or educational use. Special editions can also be created to specification.
For details, contact the Special Sales Director at the address below.

Workman Publishing Company, Inc.
225 Varick Street
New York, NY 10014-4381

Manufactured in China

10 9 8 7 6 5 4 3 2 1

FOR MY SON, BRICK

# ACKNOWLEDGMENTS

The process of publishing this book began with a one-page letter to Workman Publishing Company, containing a suggested title and a proposed format. I was fortunate. Peter Workman took my letter from a giant pile of unsolicited book proposals and placed it in a much smaller pile while personally responding that I had a "good concept and title" but he would have to see much more.

Several months later I submitted what I felt was the finished product. The book was assigned to Ruth Sullivan, my editor, for what I believed were minor corrections and polishing. Ms. Sullivan did not agree, but rather saw my work as a skeleton of what the book could and should be. Her candor, suggestions for changing content and format, and demanding professionalism made this book so much more than it was in its infancy, and to Ms. Sullivan I am sincerely thankful.

I would also like to extend thanks to my dear friends Bruce Ender and Laurie Mahan for their assistance, and to the Smith family for their encouragement and support.

# INTRODUCTION

Bring a baby to any grown-up—even the gruffest or most inhibited—and watch what happens. Without exception, they will do something to try and make the baby laugh. Psychologists, anthropologists and other experts have theories about why this is so. For me it's enough to believe that whenever a baby laughs, our humanity is somehow exalted. That is why I wrote this book.

A baby's laughter is infectious and addictive. Once you get that first little giggle, you'll do just about anything to re-create it. But it helps to have a whole repertoire of tricks. Here are 97 very silly, sometimes stupid, but effective ways to make a baby laugh—including sight gags, Laurel & Hardy routines, and parlor tricks. Most are originals developed over several years and tried out on countless babies; some are classics with a unique twist that can make the difference between a smile and a belly laugh. Among the infant-tested formulas are The Top Ten Peek-a-Boos, The

Googly Face Contest, The Live Jack-in-the-Box and that old standby, The Raspberry.

I've found that all babies will laugh at some of these skits and some babies will laugh at all of them. It's a matter of taste. Some babies delight in repetition, such as dropping an object from a high chair and having it repeatedly retrieved by Mom or Dad; others relish the unexpected, such as seeing their favorite stuffed animal transported into the room by a remote-control truck. What tickles one baby's funny bone may puzzle or even annoy another.

You will learn by trial and error what works best for your baby. The exercises in this book are geared for babies age three months (when babies first begin to have a sense of humor) to fourteen months (when their increased mobility makes them less than a captive audience). Babies as young as six months begin to appreciate incongruities. In fact, they adore them. Seeing Grandma's glasses on top of her head or the dog wearing a baby bonnet is cause for great hilarity. Or attach that rubber suction toy Baby is used to seeing on his high chair tray to your forehead and you're guaranteed a laugh.

Though the primary purpose of this book was to make babies laugh, a funny and wonderful thing happened along the way. As I experimented by having friends and relatives perform for Baby, even the most reserved would lose their inhibitions and become as goofy as their roles required. When Baby laughed, the show was a smash. But when Baby would give a deadpan reaction, the scene was often even funnier: a roomful of adults laughing hysterically at their failed attempts to make a baby laugh. Performing routines from this little book is a great way to relieve the tension and stress of life with an infant. So lighten up, rediscover your sense of the absurd, and life with Baby will be that much more fun.

# 97 WAYS TO MAKE A BABY LAUGH

# 1.

## THE LIVE JACK-IN-THE-BOX.

Put Dad in a large cardboard box. Then have the family sing the familiar tune *Pop Goes the Weasel*. When you get to the last line, Dad jumps out of the box.

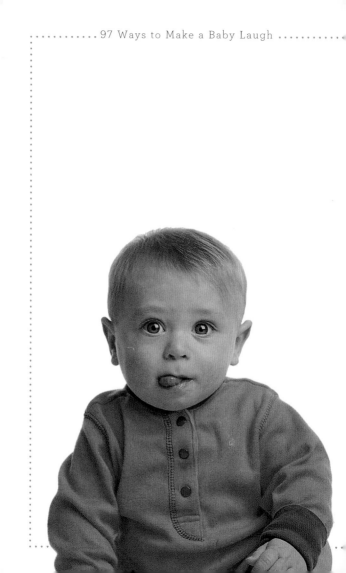

# 2.

## THE DISAPPEARING NOODLE.

Place the end of a long strand
of spaghetti in Dad's mouth
and have him suck it in as
quickly as possible.

*Note: For best results, I prefer
capellini done al dente, but I have friends
who swear by linguine.*

# 3.

## THE EXAGGERATED SNEEZE.

Fake a sneeze that takes a
long time to arrive, as in
"Ah-Ah-Ah-Ah-Choo!"

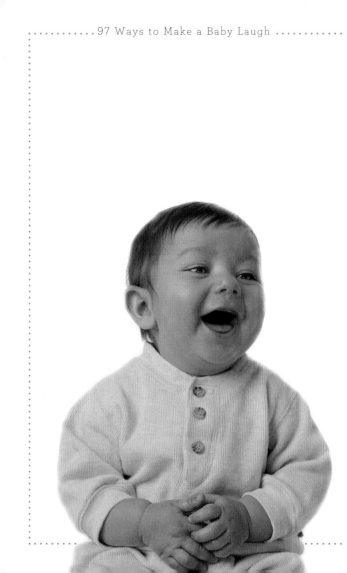

# 4.

## HOLD A SILLY FACE CONTEST.

Have family members compete for Baby's attention. Whoever gets the biggest laugh is declared the winner.

*Note: No props permitted in this one. Here's your chance to take advantage of that walleye, big nose, flexible tongue, wiggling eyebrows or any other fancy trick you've developed through the years.*

# 5.

Play rap music while Grandma does an improvisational, nonrepetitive break dance.

*Note: Everyone else in the room should clap and repeat the beat, "Go girl! Go girl!"*

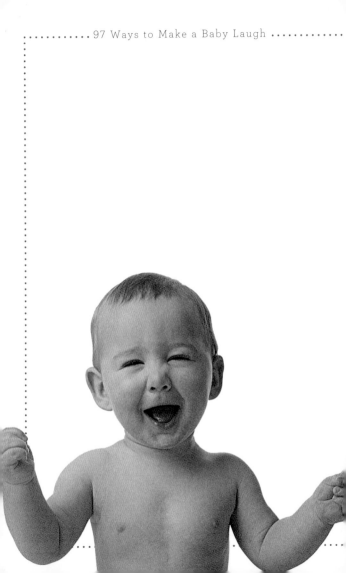

# 6.

With Baby watching, have Mom, Dad or more agile members of the family lift a soccer ball from the floor using nothing but their heads.

EQUIPMENT: *Soccer ball, floor padding*

PHYSICAL MODEL: *Irreproducible*

RISK TO PARENT: *High*

RESULTS: *Inverse ratio of parent's success to success with Baby*

# 7.

## THIS LITTLE PIGGY.

Toe play is part of every
parent's repertoire. Granted,
the original story of pigs going
to market is completely lost on
Baby, but the line "Wee Wee
Wee all the way home" rarely
fails to bring on peals
of laughter.

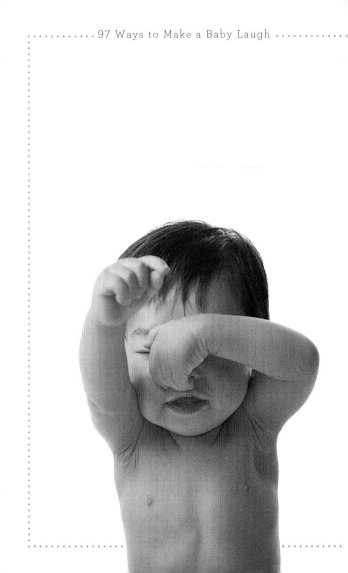

# 8.

## Peek-a-Boo 101.

Place your hands over your eyes
or over Baby's eyes. Remove
hands and say "Pee-ee-k."
A favorite version is to have
Mom hide her head beneath
a blanket and pop out at Baby
with a "Boo."

*Note: If Baby's response is deadpan,
perhaps she's too sophisticated
for basic peek-a-boo.
See Advanced Peek-a-Boo, No. 70.*

## 9.

Put on a polka
CD and do a polka with
your spouse. (But only if you
have absolutely no idea how to
actually do the polka.) There
is something inherently funny
about bad polka dancers.
Just do it.

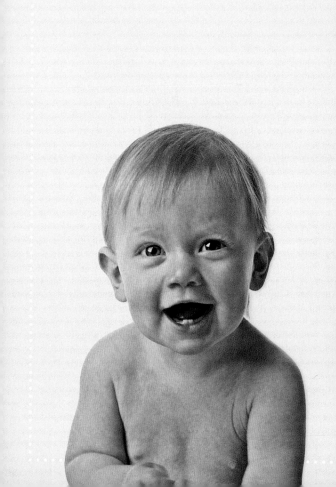

# 10.

## THE "SCAMOOCH."

This simple laugh-getter originated in Italy and was later revived for adults as "Noogies" on *Saturday Night Live*. Using the knuckles of your index and middle fingers, lightly press against Baby's ribs while jiggling your wrist. Just before doing so, say *"Somebody's gonna get a Scamooch."*

# 11.

Clear off a clean surface so there are  no other objects to distract Baby. Set up rectangular blocks with just enough space between them for a domino effect. Show Baby how to set off the chain reaction.

*Note: Given the setup time versus the payoff for this trick, it might not be a first choice for working moms.*

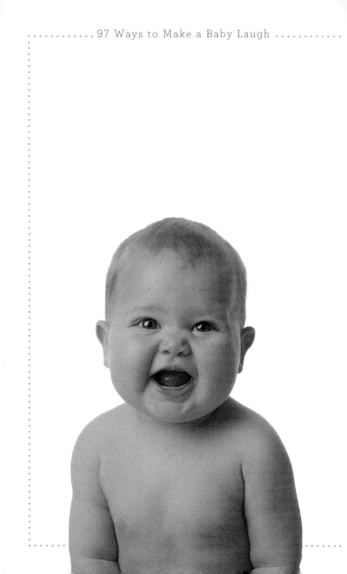

## 12.

### BABY'S STINKY FEET.

Another oldie but goodie is Baby's Stinky Feet. Put your nose close to Baby's feet, and make a face while repeating "Pee-you, Stinky" in a high-pitched voice.

*Note: "Pee-you, Stinky" gets a laugh consistently. No one knows why.*

# 13.

Blow liquid soap bubbles
through a wand for Baby.

*Note: For a real giggle, have Dad and Baby's
siblings attempt to catch the bubbles on the
tips of their noses.*

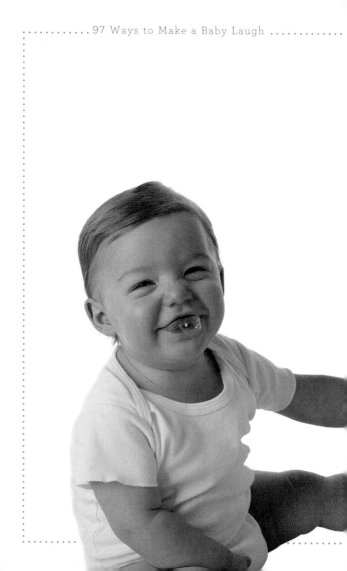

# 14.

Have everyone present do a soft-shoe while whistling the tune *Tea for Two*. Please, no substitute tunes.

*Note: Trust me on the musical selection. In the history of Hollywood movies and TV, this is the only song ever used for amateur soft-shoeing.*

# 15.

Fill a trash bag with a couple dozen colored balloons. With Baby watching from a stroller about thirty feet away from the house, release all the balloons at once from a second-story window.

*Note: Be sure Baby's head is facing the balloons at release time or you're in for a long afternoon. I learned the hard way.*

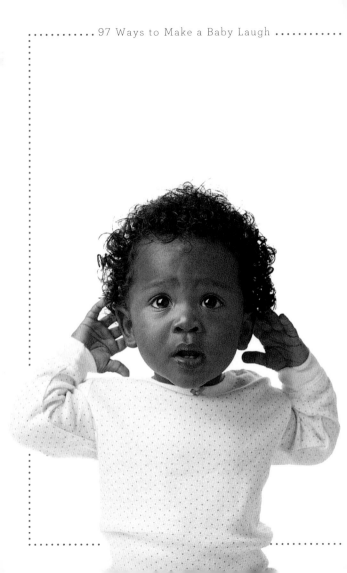

# 16.

## THE REVERSE BABY MONITOR TRICK.

When Baby is awake, reverse the transmitter and receiver of the sound monitor. Then have familiar voices address Baby from another room just before entering his view.

*Note: Our name for this electronic variation on Peek-a-Boo is Hear-a-Boo.*

# 17.

Put a baby cookie in a small bag;
put the bag in a small box;
put the box in a larger box,
and so on.
Then have each family member
open a box in Baby's view,
with Mom opening the final bag
and exclaiming
"Here's Baby's cookie!"

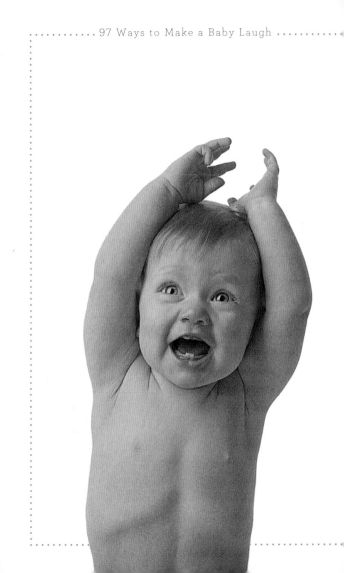

# 18.

With Baby sitting in the high
chair, hold her hands
down while you ask
"How big is Baby?"
Then, as you raise her arms
over her head, add the words
"So Big."

# 19.

Keeping your face at a safe distance from Baby, blow a large bubble gum bubble. The slower, the better.

*Note: In this trick, timing is everything.*

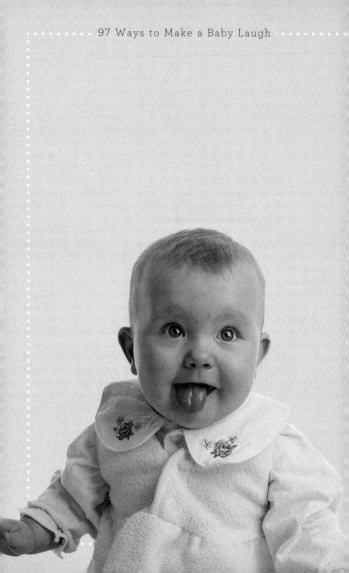

## 20.

Make a scented bubble bath for Dad, using three times the amount of soap recommended. Put Dad in the tub so that only his head is exposed above the bubbles. When the stage is set, bring Baby into the room for Show & Smell.

# 21.

## THE RASPBERRY OR BRONX CHEER.

Moisten your lips, press them lightly against Baby's arm or belly, and blow air out slowly to create a vibrating and tickling sensation. The louder and more impolite the sound, the better.

*Note: When all else fails, this old standby almost always gets a rise out of Baby.*

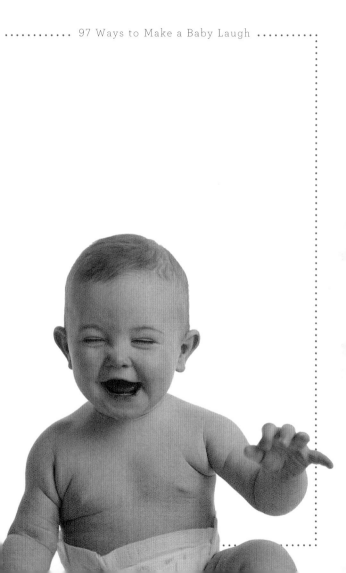

*Note: If there's no reaction, Baby is either too young or doesn't approve of streetside gambling.*

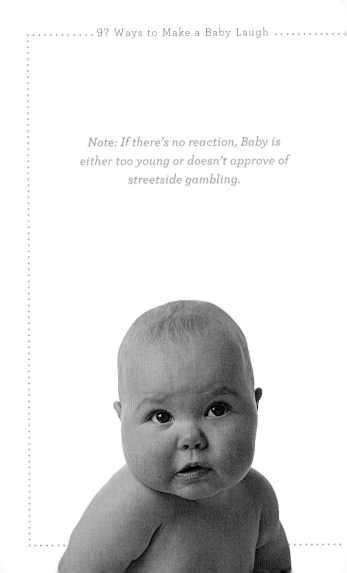

# 22.

## THREE-CARD MONTE
## FOR BABIES.

You've seen the trick where a pea
is hidden under one of three
walnut shells; the shells are
quickly shuffled around and a
player is challenged to choose
the shell that's hiding the pea.
Perform this trick for Baby
using three plastic cups and a
lemon. Applaud and make a
big fuss when Baby finds
the hidden lemon.

# 23.

Take a golf ball. Cut a hole
in the cover of a shoe box so
that the hole is just slightly larger
than the ball. Invert the cover and
assist Baby in manipulating it
until the golf ball falls
through the hole.

*Note: Every time the ball falls through the
hole, say "All gone!" in a surprised but
happy voice.*

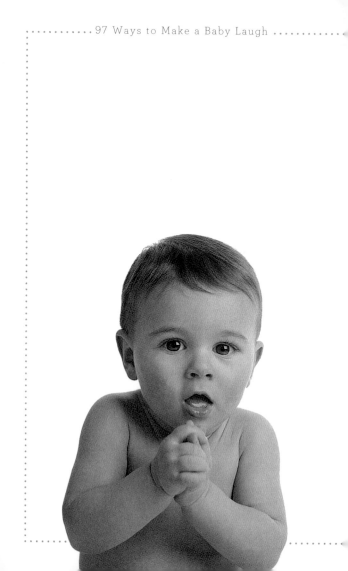

# 24.

Line up at least four people shoulder to shoulder, facing Baby. Count off 1, 2, 3, etc., starting with the person on the left. Odd-numbered players squat down while even-numbered ones stretch toward the ceiling, saying in high-pitched voices "So high!" Players then switch positions.

*Note: This scenario works best with extremely fit performers or especially bright babies.*

## 25.

Put Baby in a stroller or
high chair at the foot of
a ramp or staircase.
Roll a featherweight beach
ball down toward Baby,
beginning on the first or
second step and working your
way up. The higher you get,
the more Baby laughs.

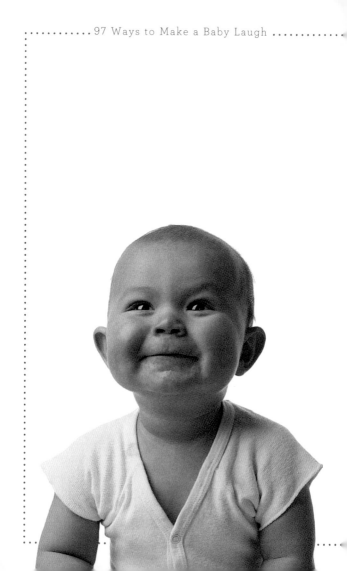

# 26.

Feed Baby from the tip of a large wooden spoon that you pretend is an airplane. Make whatever aerodynamic sounds you can think of as you loop the spoon in large circles in front of Baby. Then gently come in for a "landing" at Baby's lips.

*Note: If Baby doesn't open up for the landing, try feeding Mom or Gramps this way.*

# 27.

## BABY BINGO.

Distribute Baby's toys to a few family members. Have Mom call out names of toys as the player holding the correct toy yells out "Bingo!" and waves the toy in the air.

*Note: "Bingo" is one of the funniest and most underrated words in the English language. Yell it out a few times, and see if you don't agree.*

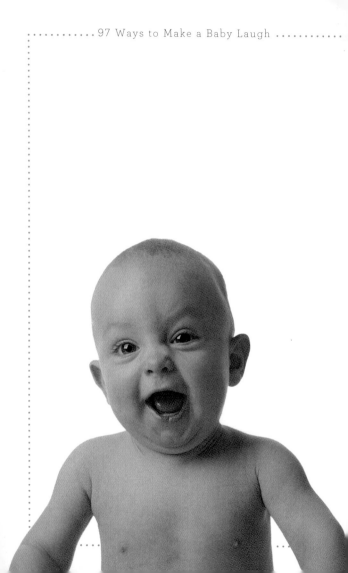

# 28.

Stage a "To-Doo To-Doo" concert using the cardboard tubes inside a paper towel or toilet tissue roll. For some unknown reason, all children naturally use these tubes as musical instruments. For a "Big Band" effect, recruit the neighbors and Baby, too.

## 29.

Dad lies on floor, faking sleep and emitting extremely loud, exaggerated snores. Each time Baby touches or pounds on Dad, he sits up in mock surprise.

*Warning: Since Baby doesn't distinguish between fake and actual sleep, Dad's catnaps are now a thing of the past.*

## 30.

Mom holds Baby on her lap facing a fully decorated Christmas tree in a dimly lit room. When she's sure Baby is looking in the right direction, someone lights the tree. This might not sound like a real thriller for you, but it's sure to get a response from Baby.

# 31.

Fill a clean spray bottle with
lukewarm water and spray
Baby's bare feet.

*Note: Some purists consider this cheating.*
*For me, it's a classic.*

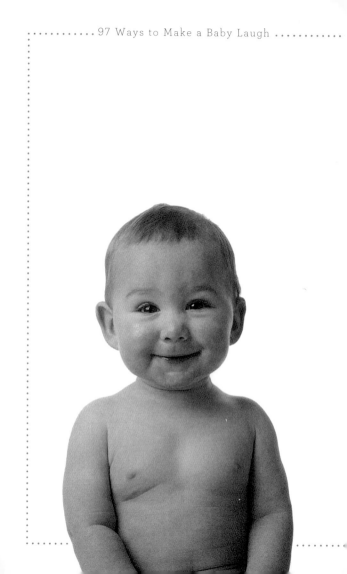

# 32.

Dampen a foam rubber or sponge animal so that it can be compressed into a tiny ball that you conceal in the palm of your hand. Turn your palm up and release the toy to its full size in front of Baby.

## 33.

Make hand puppets
by painting faces with nail
polish on old white sweat socks.
Mom and Dad can put on a
four-character show by
extending their hands and
forearms over the edge of a table
so that only the puppets are
visible to Baby.

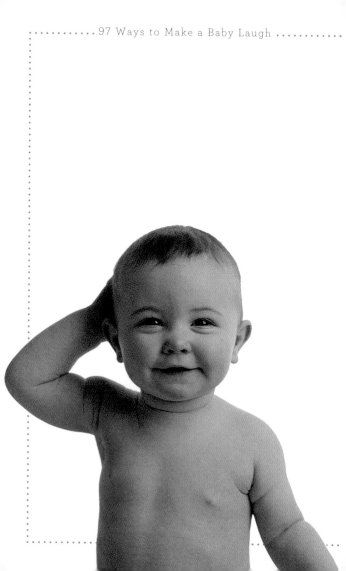

# 34.

## Two-Headed Horsey.

Mom and Dad stand back to
back, then bend forward from
the waist. A sheet draped
over their backs creates
a one-torso, two-head effect.

*Note: Some parents feel compelled to mimic
the push-me/pull-me toy when they find
themselves in this position.*

## 35.

Spice up a solo puppet act with a bit of ventriloquism. For starters, place your tongue on the roof of your mouth against your two front teeth and, without moving your mouth, say "Day-Dee" (that's ventriloquist talk for "Baby"). A mustache helps.

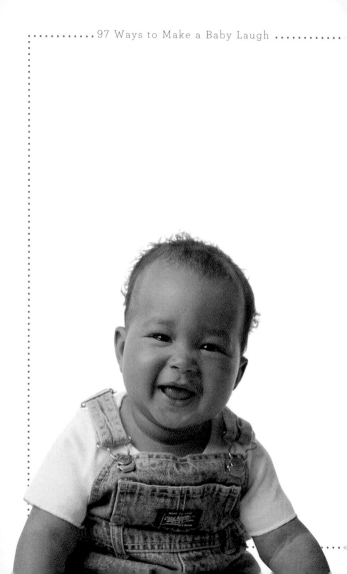

# 36.

Hold a "Barney" impression contest, with each person introducing himself to Baby with Barney's goofy, hyper-cheerful voice and flipper-like gestures.

*Note: If you don't know Barney yet, you will soon.*

## 37.

Sit down with Baby for a rerun
of *The Honeymooners* episode
in which Ralph and Ed
take mambo lessons.
Provide a baby snack for
viewing. Have Dad try
to duplicate Ralph's exact
dance steps for Baby.

## 38.

With Latin music in
the background,
form a conga line,
and parade past Baby with
Mom kicking up her heels
in front and Dad bringing
up the rear.

## 39.

Have mother-in-law use a
garden hose to spray Dad in
his bathing suit.

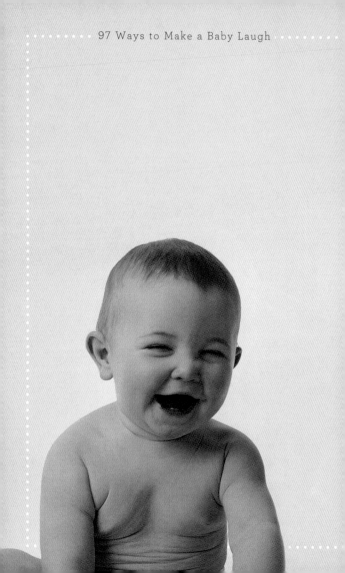

# 40.

With music playing in the background, Mom and Dad lie on the floor with feet against feet and do the bicycle exercise. Have someone start and stop the music as a cue to start and stop pedaling.

*Note: For the professional touch that Baby commands, rubber-soled shoes are a must.*

# 41.

## THE MAGNET TRICK.

You've done it before.
Now do it for Baby. Place a
metal object, such as a spoon,
on Baby's high chair tray. Drag
a magnet under the tray
so the object appears
to move unassisted.

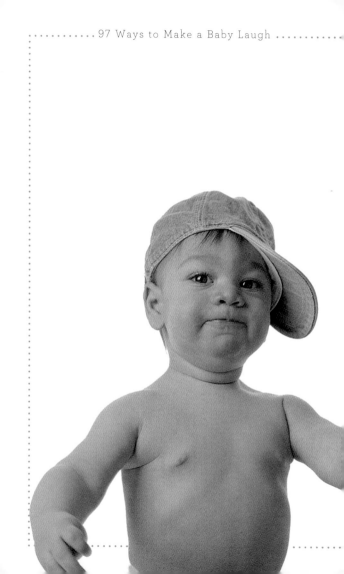

# 42.

Once Baby can sit up, bounce him on your knee to a song with a surprise ending. A good one is: *Ride away to Boston / Ride away to Lynn / You'd better watch out or / You might fall IN.*

On the last line, give a vigorous bounce, open legs and catch Baby as he drops through. After a few repetitions, Baby will start laughing in anticipation of the word "IN."

# 43.

Paste large pictures of familiar animals on sheets of paper. Players take turns choosing an animal at random, then do a sight and sound imitation of their animal for Baby. Whoever gets the biggest laugh wins.

*Note: Extra points if Baby answers back with an animal sound.*

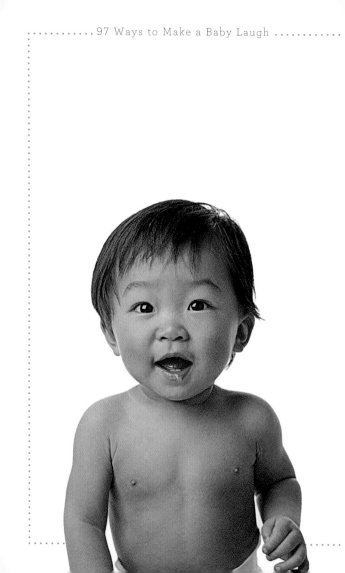

# 44.

Stage a Hawaiian hula show for Baby. Have the adult males perform in grass skirts and leis while the women sing *Here's to Baby and the Way We Do the Hula-Hoo.*

*Note: If grass skirts are unavailable, you may substitute bathing suits, but we cannot guarantee the belly laugh that the real thing elicits.*

# 45.

Bring Baby to the Laundromat
with you and let him watch
the tumbling clothes go around
in the front-load dryer.
Sound boring? Just think
back to when you thought
that tumbling clothes were
quite a sight.

# 46.

Hang Baby's favorite fluffy toy
on a rope suspended from a
tree branch, and allow her to
push the toy back and forth.
Because of the pendulum effect
and the absence of friction,
Baby's power over the toy
is greatly enhanced,
and so is her delight.

# 47.

Set a potted plant or flowers on
a phonograph turntable at a
safe distance from Baby.
Put the turntable on its
slowest speed and sing
*Ring Around the Rosy*
as the plant revolves.

*Note: For the benefit of younger parents,
a turntable is that thing in the corner of the
cellar that Mom and Dad used to play
those big vinyl records on.*

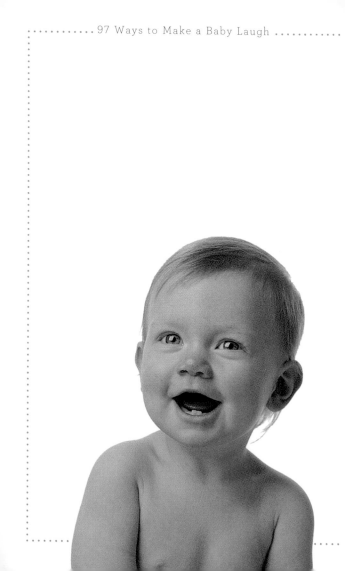

# 48.

## CHATTERING TEETH AUDITIONS.

Place a set of windup teeth
on a table. Let them chatter.
Then have family members
imitate the speed and style
of the chattering teeth.

*Note: If you don't own chattering teeth,
ask around. One of your neighbors
surely does.*

# 49.

Dress Dad and Grandpa in diapers made of sheets or white towels and give each of them a baby bottle. Have them share an afternoon snack with Baby.

*Note: Be sure to capture the moment on video or camera. The really hearty laughter will come about twenty years later.*

# 50.

## The Human Carousel.

At a playground, leave Baby
with an adult at a safe distance
from the merry-go-round.
Have family members sit at
evenly spaced seats on the
carousel, facing outward
and waving hello and good-bye
to Baby as they pass by
again and again.

# 51.

## Dinner & A Show.

While Baby is eating, have
the rest of the family perform
at the table by tapping
glasses of water with a
spoon. Make sure the glasses
have different amounts of
liquid so they will produce
a variety of tones.

*Note: Let Baby join in the fun by
playing backup percussion with a
wooden spoon on his tray.*

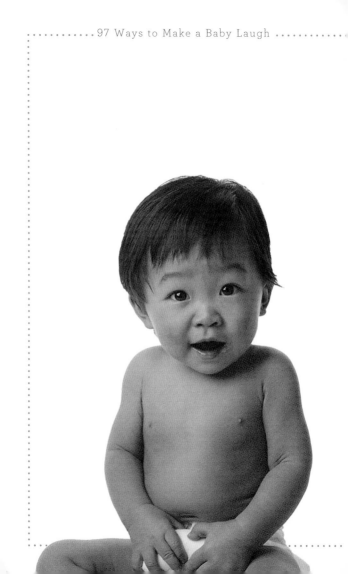

# 52.

## LIVING STATUES.

Have family dance about
the room until Mom touches
someone on top of the head,
at which point he or she freezes
in position. As Mom continues
to touch players at random,
each one is turned on and
off like a windup toy.

*Note: Baby will make the connection between
movement and Mom's touch much sooner
than you would imagine.*

# 53.

Have Dad sit, facing Baby,
with a paper cup balanced
upright on his head while
his mother-in-law fills
the cup from a pitcher.
Let Baby see at least a 12-inch
stream of water.
If Dad is especially level-headed,
pour an additional ounce or two.

EQUIPMENT: *Paper cup, pitcher, water*
PREP TIME: *Minimal*
RISK TO PARENT: *Very high*
SUCCESS RATE: *Very high*

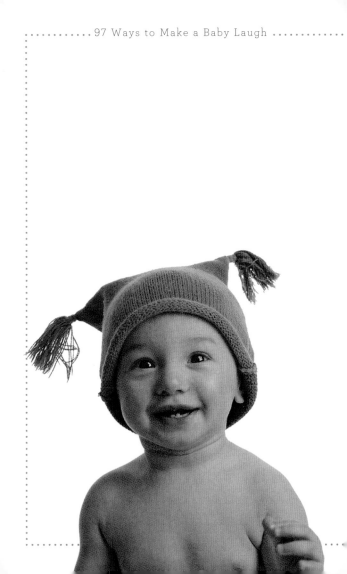

# 54.

## MIRROR, MIRROR.

Babies adore looking at
the most captivating face
of all—their own.
Hold Baby in your arms so
he's facing the mirror, point
to his reflection and say
"Look, there's Baby!"
Put one hat on you and
another on Baby. Switch hats.
Then switch them back again.

# 55.

## MECHANICAL SOLDIER.

Dad stands as stiff as a toy
soldier, with his right arm
extended straight out.
Mom pushes down the
extended arm and Dad
automatically raises his other
arm, as if mechanically. Repeat.
Baby will catch on, and you
will get a laugh eventually.

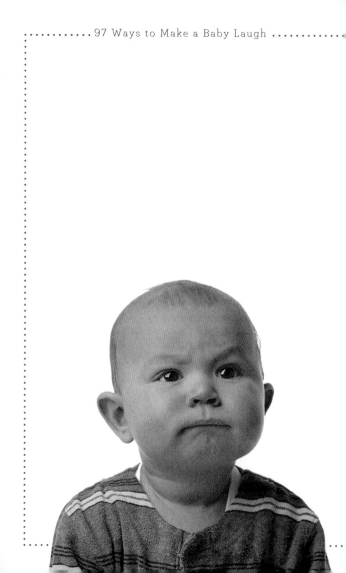

# 56.

Stage a water pistol fight among all family members in full view of Baby, but at a safe range. For a multicolor production, use a different food coloring in each of the pistols.

*Note: This game is for the truly committed— or the desperate.*

## 57.

Set Baby in front of the computer and turn on the screensaver. The Flying Toasters, the Lawn Mower and the random moving patterns of Bliss will stimulate and amuse Baby.

*Note: If you're techno-nerds, try a non-broadcasting TV station for the black-and-white snow and patterns that used to amuse the flower children of the '60s for hours.*

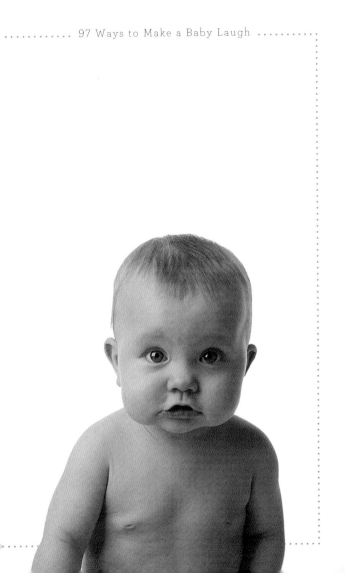

# 58.

Punch small holes near the
bottom of an empty milk
carton. As Baby watches,
fill the carton with water to
create a shower effect.

*Note: The best place to enjoy this is the tub.
Hold the carton high to make "rain" on Baby.*

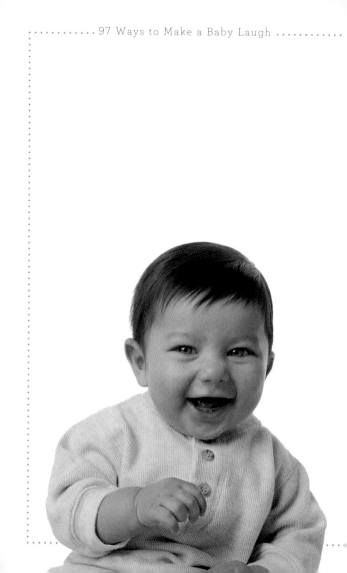

# 59.

## I'm Gonna Get You.

From about ten feet away, move slowly toward Baby wiggling your fingers and repeating, "I'm gonna GET you," before tickling. Be sure to emphasize the word "get."

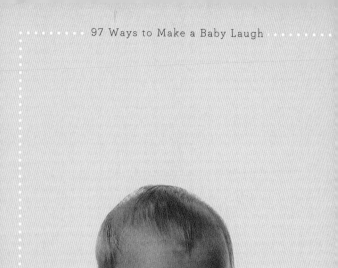

# 60.

Draw a simple cartoon face
on a sturdy piece of
cardboard. Cut a hole where
the mouth would be.
When Mom is feeding Baby,
have Dad conceal an empty
bowl behind the cardboard so
that Mom can "feed" the
cartoon face in between
spoonfuls for Baby.

# 61.

Have Grandmother squirt
whipped cream into Dad's
face whenever Baby
makes a vocal sound.
Continue until Baby laughs
or can is empty—whichever
comes first.

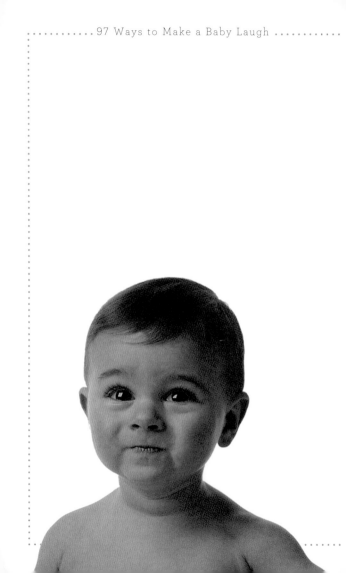

## 62.

Wet a small cloth with
vanilla extract and allow Baby
to smell it.
Baby's response will vary from
slight smile to laugh,
but it's a great forecaster of
Baby's future interest in
Häagen-Dazs and Ben & Jerry's.

# 63.

Have several people blow
New Year's Eve noisemakers
(you know, the kind that expand
in and out with your breath)
in Baby's direction.
Depending on Baby's taste, she
might prefer the all-in-unison
sound, the left-to-right
chain reaction, or the jazzier
random-order improv.

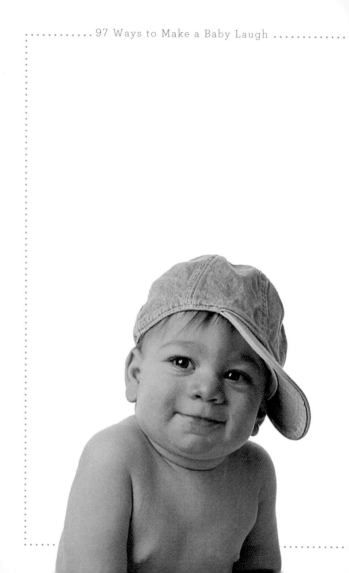

# 64.

## TREASURE HUNT.

Bury Dad in sand up to his neck and seat Baby next to his head. Baby will take it from there.

*Note: Remove all potentially dangerous objects from reach, since Baby will naturally amuse himself by taking a few swipes at Dad.*

# 65.

Put three hats on three people
in Baby's view. Then jingle a
bell—any bell will do.
Each time the bell rings,
the players quickly exchange
hats, in clockwise order.

*Note: My own extensive testing shows that a
combination of sombrero, yarmulke and any hat
with attached earmuffs works best.*

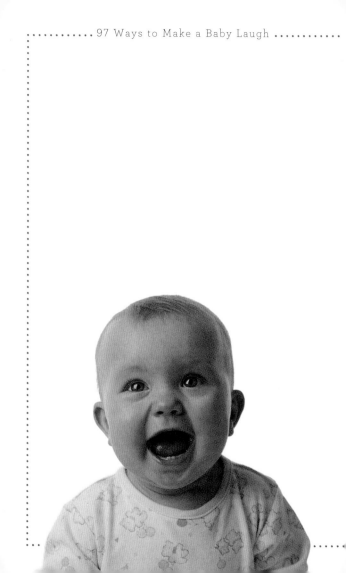

# 66.

On a large bed, allow Baby
to crawl a few feet away from you.
Then grab her legs and gently pull
her back to her starting position.
Most babies will continue
their efforts, laughing harder
with each repetition.

*Note: Some parents objected to this game,
saying that it was conditioning Baby to
the hopelessness of the human condition.
Try not to read too much into these skits—
we're just trying to get a laugh.*

# 67.

Bring Baby in for a ringside seat
as Dad sings *a cappella* in
his morning shower.
Baby is probably the only one
who ever has or ever will
appreciate Dad's singing.

*Note: Babies are totally indiscriminate when
it comes to singing. In fact, the more off-key,
the better. The more repetitious, the better.*

# 68.

Have anyone who remembers
do his best impression of
Al Jolson singing *Rock-a-Bye
Your Baby with a Dixie Melody.*

*Note: For those who have only a passing
familiarity with Al Jolson, I promise you,
without hesitation, that someone in your
extended family does this impression,
though he may not be able to get
down on his knees.*

## 69.

## I'M GONNA GET YOU, PART II.

Dad approaches Baby, saying
*"I'm gonna bite you!"*
Baby sticks hand in Dad's
mouth. Dad bites down softly
without fully closing.
Baby withdraws hand and
laughs victoriously.

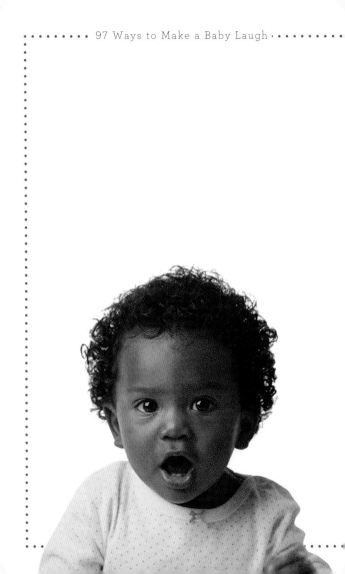

# 70.

## ADVANCED PEEK-A-BOO.

Gather several of Baby's favorite people in an adjoining room. Open and close the door, but each time have a different person behind the door say "Boo!" The unexpected changes will delight Baby.

*Note: Limit this game to doting relatives. It's not likely to go over big with guests at your Saturday night cocktail party.*

# 71.

A dripping faucet might
drive you crazy, but Baby
will think it's a hoot.
Simply allow your faucet
to drip into a half-filled
bowl of water within
Baby's sight and hearing.
Try to adjust the drops
to every two or three seconds.

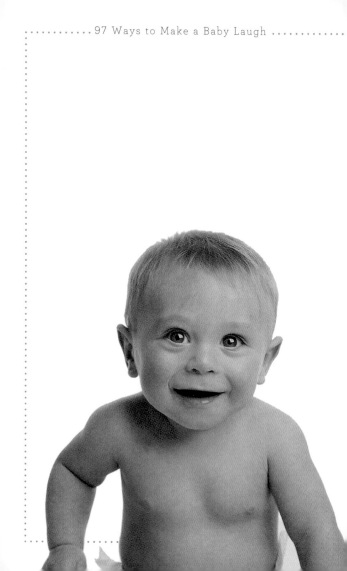

## 72.

Have Dad feed Baby from
a spoon held in the
hand of one of his
larger dolls or teddy bears.

## 73.

### BABY MAGIC.

Tie a string of bright-colored silk kerchiefs end-to-end—the more, the better. Have Dad insert them up his jacket sleeve and let Baby tug the continuous line of silk through Dad's palm.

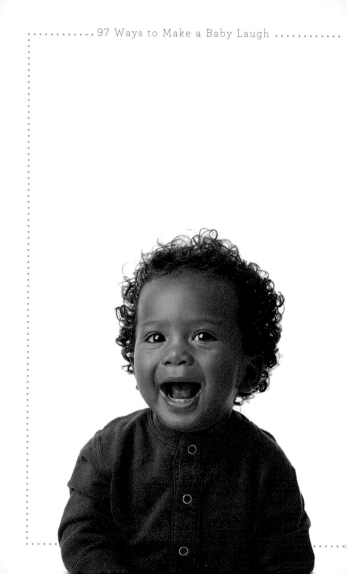

# 74.

Tie a shoe to each of the ends of two broomsticks. With the shoes dangling, move the sticks to create a dancing feet effect for Baby. Try a slow shuffle, a tap dance.

*Note: Though Baby's booties work just fine, you're apt to get a bigger laugh using Dad's or Granddad's brown wing tips.*

# 75.

Outside of Baby's view,
place a teddy bear on a
remote-control truck.
(If you don't have one, your
neighbor's son does.)
Then have the truck transport
teddy into and out of Baby's
field of vision. With each
return trip, sing out
"Look who's coming to visit."

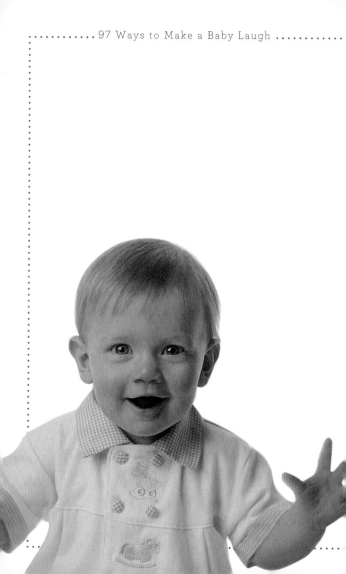

# 76.

Spread confetti over a smooth, flat surface, such as a coffee table. Once you have Baby's attention, vacuum the confetti, using the hose without attachments. Baby will marvel at the disappearing effect.

# 77.

## DOUBLE TAKE.

The "double take" is a comic delayed reaction perfected by Dean Martin and Jerry Lewis. Have one person lift a toy into the field of peripheral vision of another while the other performs his best double take.

*Note: Baby will never tire of this sight gag and will develop his own version by the time he's old enough to talk.*

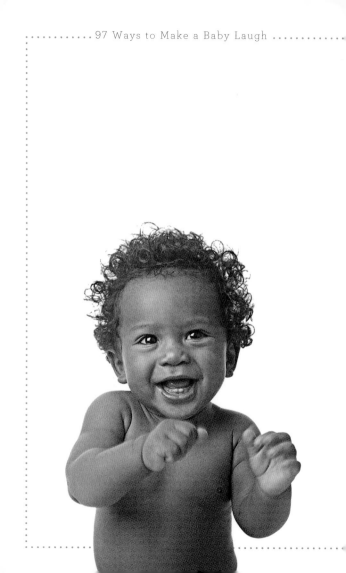

# 78.

## RIDE 'EM COWBOY.

Baby watches as Mom
rides on the back of Dad,
who is crawling on all fours.

*Note: Though Baby has never seen
a Western, "Gitty-Ups," "Yahoos" and
hat-waving are a must.*

# 79.

Using a large, clear plastic
glass filled with water, blow
continuous air bubbles
through a straw.
All kids, from babies through
middle-school children,
love this effect and begin
imitating it at an early age.

*Note: Baby will also enjoy watching you
blow bubbles with a straw in his bathwater.*

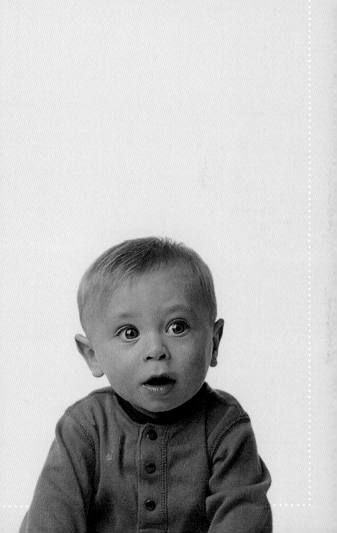

*Note: A giant plastic bat makes
the perfect prop,
but a straw broom will do.*

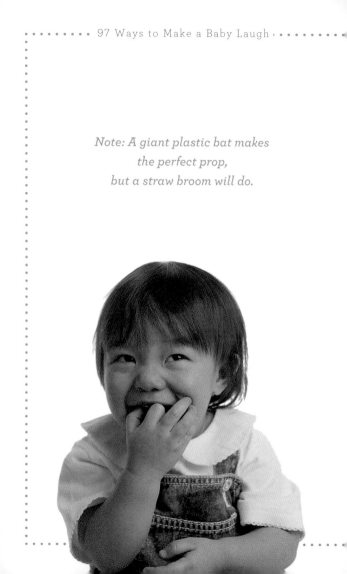

# 80.

## THE WHITE CLOWN AND ROGUE CLOWN ACT.

This was a favorite stock routine in French and Italian circuses. Every time the Rogue Clown bends over to pick up an object, he receives a whack on the rear end from the sophisticated White Clown, which interrupts his effort. Mom and Dad don't need the clown outfits to act this out for Baby.

# 81.

Blow up a balloon.
Stretch the end of the
mouthpiece to allow
the air to screech out.
Vary the pitch by
stretching the mouthpiece
to different lengths.

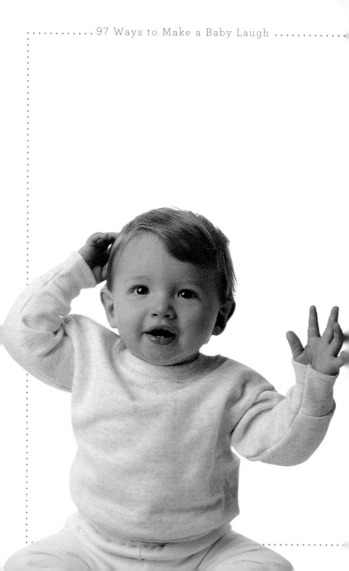

# 82.

## Shadow Play.

In a darkened room, shine a flashlight against the wall. Position Baby so that the spontaneous movement of her arms will create shadows. Baby will enjoy the moving patterns even if she doesn't yet connect them to her own body movements.

*Note: The only problem you might encounter here will be Dad's or Granddad's insistence on doing "rabbit ears." Avoid this problem by providing them with their own flashlight and wall.*

# 83.

Turn a fur-lined glove inside out and allow Baby to feel its softness. Then tie a string to the glove, and cause it to move along the floor or table to create a lifelike impression. Make meowing or barking sounds depending upon the size of the glove.

*Note: Though our fur glove bit got at least a smile from the majority of babies tested, we met a few precocious nine-month-old animal rights activists who want nothing to do with this trick.*

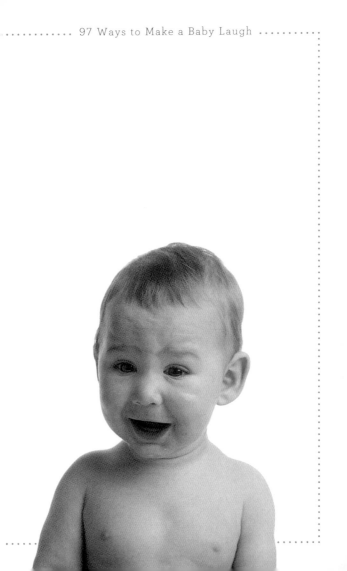

*Note: We've had at least two reports of Dads who went on yodeling for years, causing ostracism from family and neighborhood gatherings.*

## 84.

### YODELING IN THE CANYON.

With Baby on Mom's lap,
Dad stands across the room
and lets out a resonant
"Yodel-ay-he-hoo!"
Use the classic Swiss
four-repetition method until
Baby becomes so familiar
with Dad's falsetto voice that
the yodel consistently
brings a smile.

# 85.

## TONGUE TEASERS.

Stick your tongue out slowly
as far as you can—no more than
a quarter-inch per second. Pull
tongue back at the same speed.
Then repeat the motion, this
time as quickly as possible.
Alternate the methods.

*Note: We know you'll do anything to amuse Baby,
but we strongly suggest that you NOT practice
this technique on buses or subways—
or on the job.*

# 86.

## Do a "Danny."

(If Mom and Dad are too young to remember this sight gag from *The Danny Thomas Show,* ask Grandpa to demonstrate.) Take a mouthful of water. Then, acting as if Baby has just made you laugh, turn away and eject the water. With a little practice, you will master the art of emitting a fine, evenly distributed spray with the timing that would make even Danny proud.

# 87.

## Snake-in-the-Grass.

Stretch a long piece of rope on the ground. Have a person at each end wiggle the rope from side to side so that a series of "waves" is created. Vary the size of the waves to make the snake appear to move faster or slower.

*Note: If you've forgotten how to do this, have any kids in the neighborhood demonstrate for Baby. They all know how.*

## 88.

Submerge two different-colored rubber or plastic balls in a tub of water. Release the balls to the surface one at a time, so that only one ball is ever visible to Baby.

# 89.

Fill a large laundry bag with Baby's stuffed animals and toys. Bring the bag to Baby and present each toy with great fanfare.

*Note: Since Baby cares only about having and holding, not owning, it will be like receiving a new bagful of gifts every time.*

# 90.

## Baby Channel Surfing.

Seat Baby in a high chair facing the TV. With close supervision, help Baby press the remote control's channel changer.

*Note: In most families, this is the only instance in which Dad will part with his remote.*

# 91.

## FETCH.

Now that Baby's here, is Mom missing those aerobic workouts? Place a beach ball on the table surface of Baby's high chair, and stand several feet away. Continue to retrieve and replace the ball until Baby tires of the game or nightfall, whichever comes first (usually the latter).

*Note: Mom, if you get bored, think of it this way: your budding Newton is experimenting with cause-and-effect relationships.*

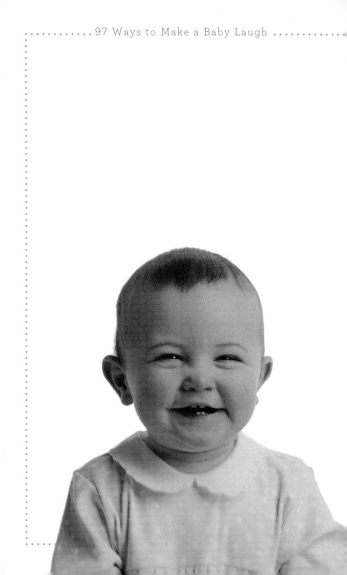

## 92.

### Using Your Noggin.

Attach a suction cup toy—like the one on Baby's high chair tray—to your forehead. Baby will find this trick—and you—a laugh riot.

# 93.

The oldest trick in the book is probably FUNNY EARS. Insert your thumbs in your ears, with your fingers outstretched and your palms facing Baby; then either wiggle your fingers or use the open-and-close method, whichever gets the bigger laugh.

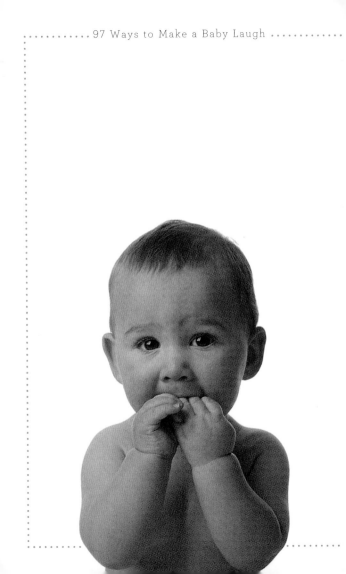

# 94.

On a summer day, stage a
water balloon toss for Baby.
After the balloons have been
filled with water and tied,
have family and friends
form two lines, facing each
other, and begin tossing.

# 95.

At a safe distance from Baby, have Dad illustrate his mastery of the pogo stick.

*Note: Depending on Dad's athletic ability, a "safe distance" could range from the width of a driveway to the length of a football field.*

# 96.

Have Dad play two notes on any
musical instrument—a keyboard
is best. Play the same two notes
over and over
as Mom sings *"Bay-bee, Bay-bee"*
to the beat. Then reverse, with
Mom accompanying Dad
in a higher key.

*Note: This one will really work; save it for
moments of true desperation.*

## 97.

Tie two helium balloons
to Grandfather's ears
on twelve-inch strings.
Dangle two sticks of
chewing gum from his upper lips
as cartoon-style teeth.
Then have Grandpa sing the
first few bars of *Be My Love*
to Baby in his best
Mario Lanza impression.

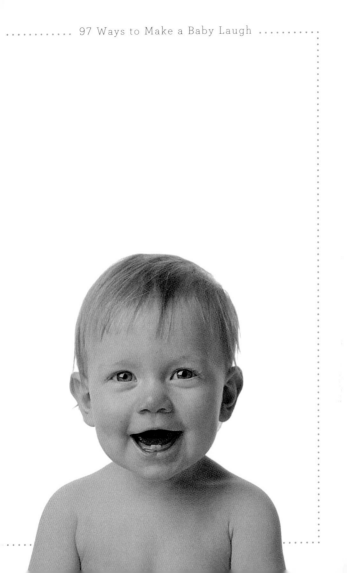

# 98.

*Insert your own
favorite laugh-getter
and Baby's picture.*

# 99.

_____

_____

_____

_____

_____

_____

*Insert your own*
*favorite laugh-getter*
*and Baby's picture.*

# ABOUT THE AUTHOR

JACK MOORE was a writer from New Jersey who was loved by all who knew him. A true polymath, Jack was as comfortable discussing philosophy as he was playing the jester. Always the children's entertainer and clown at family gatherings, he perfected his ways to make babies laugh when his son, Brick, was born. Friends and family encouraged Jack to write down his "Infant Laugh Formulas" for other parents.

# ABOUT THE BABIES

BABIES ARE THE GREATEST AUDIENCE, especially the twenty babies who humored us by sitting for their portraits and laughing at our attempts to make them laugh. So thanks to: Branden, Deklan, Hannah, Jack, Janie, Jonathan, Julian, Justin, Kelly, Killian, Liam, Lein, Michael, Nicolas, Orion, River, Ruby, Siobhan, Zachary and Zoe.

## ABOUT THE PHOTOGRAPHER

Penny Gentieu is a New York photographer who has specialized in photographing babies and children for more than 25 years. Her photographs are exhibited and published worldwide, and she has to her credit over 100 magazine covers— *Time, Newsweek, American Baby, Baby Talk, New York, USA Weekend, Parents*—and a dozen children's books.